AWAKE

Our Mental Health
Love the Conversation

AWAKE

Our Mental Health
Love the Conversation

A. J. Ormiston

ARTHUR H. STOCKWELL LTD
Torrs Park, Ilfracombe, Devon, EX34 8BA
Established 1898
www.ahstockwell.co.uk

British Library Cataloguing-in-Publication Data.
A catalogue record for this book is available
from the British Library.

ISBN 978-0-7223-5012-6
Printed in Great Britain by
Arthur H. Stockwell Ltd
Torrs Park Ilfracombe
Devon EX34 8BA

CONTENTS

FOREWORD

You say everything is okay and hide the painful truth. You feel lost, your world is falling apart. Dark thoughts and urges overwhelm you. You are struggling through the day and night. There is not a precious moment to lose. Don't be afraid to say you are not okay. You have such a kind heart, be kind on yourself too. Talk to someone now, tell them your story. They will listen and not judge you. Hold on to the belief it will get better and stay strong.

LEAP OF FAITH

I cannot face talking about myself
I want to dull the pain
Not sit with another stranger
Tell my story again

I cannot trust myself
I have heard it all before
Maybe I will just miss my bus
Walk past the open door

It is something we can do
If only we could do more
Take you to appointments
Watch you walk through the door

Wait in cafés, on street corners
Be there to see you leave
Know that you have been there
No need for stories, we believe

You need to learn to trust, hope
Take a leap of faith
Bonds you build, words of wisdom
Will help to keep you safe

Choices
You could run and hide
But stranger things have happened
Open up, step inside

THE EYES OF THE WORLD

Who are you to judge me
If you do not know what is real
Believe you have the answers
Truly understand the pain I feel

You tell me it will get better
Physical & mental scars will heal
So convinced I have the answers
Hold the key to stop the pain I feel

If only I did
The world would be a better place
All I can control just now
The blank expression on this face

Slowly turn corners, take different paths
There are closed doors you can unlock
Learn, be strong
For you cannot turn back the clock

Draw pictures, write your story
Talk and listen to trusted voices
Live in the present moment
Find calm, choices

MIRROR, MIRROR

Mirror, Mirror
Who am I, what am I
This reflection of my life
I see a grotesque, scarred shell

A true reflection
Or what you want to see
Just imagine
Be anything you want to be

BELIEVE, YOU CAN

Why do I have no purpose in life
i don't really know when it all began
Feeling hopeless and worthless
No plan

Why does there need to be a sense of purpose
Who really has a master plan
Live life to the full
You are invaluable, loveable
Believe, you can

DEFUSED

It feels like there is a bomb waiting to go off
I hold the pin
Everyone around me would be blown into pieces
Broken hearts, crushed souls
My mental torture

The things you never said or revealed
Written down, pictures – too late
Pain that is gone and left behind
For others to seek answers and somehow understand
Hold on

Darkness and light, love and hate
I am so confused
Think, think, choices, consequences
I am not alone, defused

MESSAGES [1]

Lost, I can see the sky
Touch the ground
I am not missing me
Not sure if I want to be found

Seconds can turn into minutes and hours
When all hope feels like it has gone
Please, please send now to anyone
'I'm here' –

Messages

BLISS

We can't help asking 'How are you'
And we know you will say 'I'm okay'
We know you think we don't believe you
But what else do you expect us to say

I know if I say 'I don't know'
They will ask me is that the truth
And I will just put on my angry voice
I cannot offer any proof

It would be great to just say 'I'm not okay'
And that's just the way it is
No third degree, interrogation
Bliss

EGGSHELL

Treading on the world's largest eggshell
Not knowing, what is the right thing to say
Are we making it worse
Just hoping you will be better one day

It will take time to fix the cracks
I know you try to be careful what you say
I know you love me, be patient
Just be there and I will be okay

WAITING BY THE PHONE

My mind is on the screen
I wait for the next post
Pictures, words, moving images
I could like, love, laugh
I can be engaging, comment, smile
Feel numb, keep scrolling

Search for the real you
Find your true friends, in all the connections
Don't tap, talk
Make it happen

THE DOORSTEP

You stand on the doorstep
You are, where you are
A mind full of mixed memories and experiences
Close doors behind you

I open the gate that has kept me in, others out
The road outside goes downhill and uphill
That doesn't matter
I think whichever way I go, I will be okay.

YOU SAID YOU WERE FINE

You sat there
I could see you, reach out and touch
I think this made me feel better
I worry so much

As you headed out, I so wanted to believe
Your smile means everything to me
You said you were fine
We next met in A & E

Out of the darkest of nights
Light begins to shine through sad eyes
I think I can feel it emerging
I no longer need a disguise

DARK CLOUDS

I need to find a shelter from the storm
Somewhere that keeps me dry
Where I feel safe
As thunder and lightning pass by

Dark clouds
It's not always going to rain
But I know it will pour down on me
Before there are blue skies again

If you get soaked love
When despite it all, rain gets in
The warmth and love around you
Will dry your delicate skin

FIND

You took a flight to anywhere and nowhere
Lost in some faraway place
Far from what we call home
Find your bearings
The compass in your shoe
Fix yourself on the horizon
Feel where the sun hits your face
The world is your oyster
You will find your rightful place

THE ELEPHANT

In the room, I know what it is
But words fail me
And I don't know why.
The kindest open invite
To say whatever is on my mind
Without fear of consequence.
What could be worse than how I feel.
Speak now, speak now, speak now
What stops me.

Nothing could be worse than how we feel.
Helpless,
As you carry such a heavy weight on your own.
Speak now
All we will do is listen
All we can promise is our unconditional love
Work out with you the next step,
A beginning.

A NEW BEGINNING

I tell myself it is a new beginning
I know I may falter
But really believe I am winning

I know I am not unique
Many other people struggle to cope
Win battles
Never give up hope

You are so strong, you are here
Despite all you have been through
And with sword and shield
Will be our love for you

AWAKE

Through the gate
Everyone who wonders is not lost
Tree-lined paths provide order
Follow the stream
Talk about everything and nothing, it's unconditional
'Good morning', good people pass by
The young cygnets protected as they grow
Swim in the big pond
Poppies and sunflowers colour this world
Mind the nettles
It can all make sense
So natural and simple
Awake